SNOW BONES

Snow Bones

Masaya Saito

ISOBAR
PRESS

First published in 2016 by

Isobar Press
Sakura 2-21-23-202, Setagaya-ku,
Tokyo 156-0053, Japan
&
14 Isokon Flats, Lawn Road,
London NW3 2XD, United Kingdom

http://isobarpress.com

ISBN 978-4-907359-15-7

ACKNOWLEDGEMENTS

A few of these haiku have previously appeared
in *Ash* (TELS Press, 1988), in the journals *Modern Haiku*
and *Wingspan,* and in the anthologies *Haiku World: An
International Poetry Almanac* (Kodansha International,
1996) and *Haiku in English: The First Hundred Years*
(Norton, 2013); Japanese versions of some of the
pieces have appeared in *Asahi Shimbun, Haiku,
Haiku Asahi,* and *Haiku Bungei.*

CONTENTS

SNOW BONES: remnants of snow after a thaw; patches of snow seen stretching along ridges, in ruts, or in furrows, &c., after a partial thaw.

for my parents

prologue

A cold sunset

on the cliff, me
without wings

urn

I

Snow shoveled
from the roof

blue sky silence

Winter carp
huddled together

one of them, red

White breath

my last day
unknown

No alternative
but to walk away

a frozen rock

Across the snowfield

my footprints
each one, deep

In the distance
a house on fire

my arms, crossed

Nameless

each mountain
asleep

Plodding further
through snow

inhabiting the sound

The old bull's bellow

from behind
the thatch snowshield

My snow boots

huge, step over
the threshold

The old house

tick
of a pendulum

Feeble earthquake

a paper doll
still standing

Winter seclusion

I caress
a gourd's waist

Sleeping alone

inside the pillow
a blizzard

II

From behind the shoji screen
my mother calls

spring

The rice-pounding mallet
swung high

the blue sky

Flying a kite

its tug
in my fist

The stud bull's
bellow

the thaw begins

Night coming on

a patch of snow
in the roadside mirror

Here in this darkness

shared
with a cat in heat

Awake
in spring dawn

the sound of water

A balloon
tied by its cord

breeze

A seedling
drops soil

on soil

A leap
over spring mud

towards Mother

III

Suddenly, she's a Buddha

a rice cake
stuck in her throat

Spring dawn

the corpse
remains a corpse

Caressing her dead face

the chin
with its wart

Looking into
the coffin's window

in front of the furnace

Light makeup
on her face

spring cold

Cremation

smoke disappears
into the blue sky

Out of the furnace

the bones still
preserve her shape

Lingering cold

the funeral procession
passes a utility pole

My hands
numb with cold

in prayer

The funeral over

the sound
of tatami-sweeping

IV

The paper doll
fallen

the house, quiet

A pair of glasses
a keepsake

spring cold felt again

Rice cakes soaking

scooping one up
I disturb the water

Hazy night

something soft
I want to grab

Soap bubble
gone

blue sky

A swallow enters
the barn's darkness

noon

I take down
the thatch snowshield

the house breathes

Through the window
my father hoeing

darker and darker

three voices:
   metropolis

first voice

Here comes
a balloon

amid the countless faces

A long day

a bronze Hercules
drawing his bow

The fountain
stays low

preserving its strength

The swing, abandoned,
still swaying

noon

Cherry blossoms

darkness
within my mouth

The crowds

connected by
a spring bridge

Turning a corner
he disappears

with the balloon

second voice

I hold its string

the balloon strains
already in the sky

Serene as ever

the balloon
begins to rise

The balloon rising higher

behind the windows
people working

Center of the sky

too far
even for the balloon

Forever singular

the balloon
rising still higher

As if sinking

the balloon in the deeper
and deeper sky

third voice

Spring night

whose lingering perfume
in the elevator

Clean shaven
I'm lonely

in the mirror

Insomnia

loving snakes
more than God

Awaking
from a spring dream

my throat, parched

The watch
cold on my wrist

I leave for the office

A poorly-paid job
which I suffer daily

water grows warmer

Departing spring

documents
piled up like a fort

At an office window

how red
that balloon rising

three voices:
countryside

first voice

Waking from a nap

an old man
in the mirror

Still poor
still unmarried

I wash my face

An insect cage

a cricket's feeler
protruding

A musty hut

going out, I turn the key
in the tiny lock

Clean shaven

walking through
the deserted village

Barbed wire fence

smell
of rampant grass

Off the path
even further

my butterfly net

A parasol

or so it seems
up there on the brink

Through the tunnel

echo
of each footstep

Sweltering sky

the deserted school's
silent loudspeaker

The cicadas are shrieking

I can't see
any of them

Shimmering
in heat haze

I walk on

A swarm of mosquitoes

passing through it
evening sunlight

Fireflies flitting

not enough
to call a swarm

second voice

This house, quiet

I keep
a single goldfish

Barefoot

across the tatami floor
across the wooden floor

In a shoe
I was about to put on

an ant crawling

Opening my parasol

the sound
deep in my ears

Through the tunnel

my parasol
closed

From here on

the path
straight to the edge

On the cliff now

down there
a butterfly net

Perspiring slightly

myself
silence

Moving backwards
a few steps

I leave the edge behind

Nothing to do

my footsteps beneath
the sweltering sky

Water drips
from a crack in rock

one drop on my palm

Lotus pads

on each one
air

Cicadas shrieking

the thatched house
grows still older

Returning

my face
in the mirror

Sunset glow

the pendulum
motionless

Moonlight

folded into
a paper crane

In this house
where my sister is the wife

a firefly cage

Pregnant
my sister squats

holding a sparkler

third voice

Verdurous night

me
in this large chair

Lust

made flesh
would be a toad

My wife conceived
that full moon night

or so it seems

Sleeping
my head pointed north

a sunflower in my dream

Awaking

forlorn
I put away the futon

Morning chill

my voice
from within

This house, quiet

a peach
begins to decay

My anger restrained

a red rose in the vase
one petal falls

An empty plate

smashing it
autumn clearer

My thoughts tangled

I cross
the threshold

A molting rooster

reflected
in the roadside mirror

My shadow approaches
a praying mantis

covering its shadow

Through a flower field
comes a man

with one arm

Balmy autumn

a sundial
at the deserted school

A forked road

both left and right
autumn evening

A misty night

I exist
as footsteps

urns

I

No handcuffs
no leg-irons

basking in the sun

To live
is to move

a winter sparrow

From slum to slum

I cross
a cold bridge

Somewhere
in the flea market

a cellphone ringing

Runny nose

my hometown
so distant

Office buildings

turning a corner
a sudden chill

Underground city
so bright, so bright

flu coming on

Holding the train strap

this year
about to end

In the long-distance train
a conversation overheard

my dialect

On the overhead rack
my winter hat

on its way north

II

Home

heavy futon
heavy darkness

My father asleep
grinding his teeth

so cold

Awaking from
a New Year dream

a hollow in the pillow

A shadow
cast on a shoji screen

opens it

A flu mask

through it my father's
heavy dialect

The abrupt sound
of tearing off the cover

the brand new calendar

A single leek

longer than
the cutting board

A winter egg

I crack it
in this large house

Watched

a rice cake
is slow to swell

Licking up winter sunlight

a wasp
begins to walk

From upstairs
far into the withered field

a paper plane

How cold

my chest
against the desk edge

My pen
still motionless

heavy kimono

Snow falling
quietly

already afternoon

Father's footsteps

upstairs, faint
in this winter house

'Stand up straight!'

I shake
the straw charcoal sack

Across a snowfield

my footprints
each one, deep

Hometown barbershop

in the mirror
snow falling

On a stump
a dome of snow

blue sky

The snowfield

I retrace
my own footsteps

Walking across the dirt floor

my boots
spill snow

As if sulking

a rice cake
begins to swell

In a heavy kimono
this old poet

no longer flaps his wings

Chill after a bath

the tick
of a pendulum

Nightcap

ambition
hard to abandon

III

The paper screen

behind it
my father's body

The futon
humped

dead hands in prayer

The chief mourner
the only son

I shovel the snow

Hot sake at the wake

a hoarse voice
'Hold your life dear!'

The coffin departs

tire tracks
in the snow

The futon
on which my father died

hurled into the flames

Numb with cold

I hold a piece of bone
with long chopsticks

Footprints
across the snowfield

my dead father's

In mourning

letting the icicles
grow

Earmuffs off

this house
quiet

A single cord

I pull it, brighten
the cold evening

Cold water
poured on a knife

I begin to sharpen it

The blade enters

a voiceless
sea slug

Whispering
a ball-bouncing song

home alone

Freezing, mouth agape
taking medicine

still unmarried

Winter mirror

how quickly
my face grows old

In the snow country
my parents gone

a pendulum swinging

IV

Blue sky

I uncross
my arms

Waterless river

I walk
along the bank

A flu mask

a passer-by's mumble
perhaps a greeting

Standing still

surrounded by
winter trees

As I draw closer

a fox in a trap
moves

The snowfield

those gravestones
crowded together

A visit to a grave

a candle flame
shielded with my hand

Hands together in prayer

now apart, ready
to leave my hometown

Lifting my feet high
right and left

I cross the snowfield

Vying for length
in silence

icicles

Breaking off an icicle

to stab
the snow

epilogue

Driving away

in the rear-view mirror
a cold sunset

CPSIA information can be obtained
at www.ICGtesting.com
Printed in the USA
BVOW09s0858230218
508704BV00001B/44/P